Acknowledgement ix

153 - The Perfect Catch 1

ONE - A Conversation between the Father, the Son, and the Holy Spirit 6

FIVE - Adam, Solomon & a Scientist 9

THREE - A Conversation between God, the Devil and Man 13

The Divine Promise and the Sacred Journey of His People 18

A Conversation Between Isaiah, Jeremiah, and John the Baptist 23

The Gathering of Five: A Conversation Across Time 27

The Profound Significance of the Number Five in Jesus' Ministry 30

The Significance of the Number Three in the Ministry of Jesus 33

The Divine Significance of Numbers 1, 3, and 5 in the Ministry of Jesus' Disciples 36

Symbolism of 153 41

Acknowledgement

Jesus Christ is the very foundation of my existence, the light that has illuminated my path for over 80 years. Under His divine protection and boundless grace, I have journeyed through life, strengthened by His unfailing love. Born and raised in the historic town of Patna, India, I faced many trials and adversities—especially the weight of discrimination for being a Christian. Yet, through every challenge and questioning glance, my Lord stood by me, guiding me with His wisdom and filling my heart with an unshakable faith. For this, I bow before Him in eternal gratitude.

My heart overflows with thankfulness for my beloved family—my pillar of strength and joy. To my dearest wife, Avis, whose unwavering support and encouragement have been my greatest source of inspiration, I owe more than words can express. To my four sons and their loving wives, each of whom has enriched my life in their unique way, I extend my deepest appreciation. And to my six precious grandchildren, whom I cherish dearly—I pray that this book finds its way into your hands and that it strengthens your faith, just as the Word of God has strengthened mine.

Over the years, my love for the Holy Scriptures has only deepened. Among the countless passages that have touched my soul, one verse stood out profoundly—John 21:11, the miraculous account of the 153 large fish. This divine revelation stirred something within me, urging me to share my reflections with the world. When I confided in my wife, Avis, she encouraged me wholeheartedly, just as she has done at every step of my life's journey.

I am deeply grateful to my eldest son, Shailendra, who once remarked on how my thoughts and insights are a gift from God—words that affirmed my calling to write. My second son, Amitabh, residing in London, has not only been a source of encouragement but has also helped refine my biblical writings with his keen editorial eye. My third son, Amit, with whom I now reside, continually uplifts me with his kindness and patience, standing by me as I navigate the challenges of old age and frail health. And my youngest son, Rohit, has been instrumental in editing and publishing all my books, including this one. Thanks to him, my works — **"I Love You"** and **"The Conclusion"** —are now available to readers worldwide.

God's presence is my greatest treasure, and as long as I have breath, I pray that He will continue to inspire me to share His teachings. May this book be a vessel of His truth, touching hearts and drawing souls closer to His everlasting love.

153 – The Perfect Catch

The morning mist still clung to the waters of the Sea of Galilee as Simon Peter and his companions pulled in their empty nets. The night had been long, and despite their efforts, they had caught nothing. Thomas, Nathanael, James, and John sat in the boat, exhausted, staring at the rippling waves. Their hearts were heavy—not just from the failed catch but from everything that had happened.

Jesus had died. And though He had risen, things were no longer the same. Peter, once so bold, now felt lost. He had denied his Master three times, and guilt weighed on his soul. What else could he do now but return to what he knew best—fishing? The others followed, uncertain of their future.

As dawn broke, a figure stood on the shore. His voice carried over the waters, gentle yet firm:

"Friends, have you caught anything?"

Peter shook his head. "Nothing."

"Throw your net on the right side of the boat, and you will find some."

The men exchanged glances. They had heard this before—years ago, when Jesus first called them to be fishers of men. Could it be…?

John's eyes widened in recognition. He turned to Peter and whispered, **"It is the Lord!"**

Peter's heart pounded. Without a second thought, he plunged into the water and swam toward the shore. The others followed in the boat, dragging the net full of fish.

As they reached land, they saw a fire burning. Fish were already laid out, and bread was waiting. Jesus, smiling, gestured for them to bring some of their catch.

"Come and have breakfast," He said.

They ate in silence, overwhelmed with awe. Then Jesus turned to Peter, His eyes filled with love.

"Simon, son of John, do you love Me?"

Peter looked down, ashamed, remembering his denial. "Yes, Lord, You know that I love You."

"Feed My lambs," Jesus said.
Again, Jesus asked, "Simon, son of John, do you love Me?"

Peter's heart ached. "Yes, Lord, You know that I love You."

"Take care of My sheep."
A third time, Jesus asked, "Simon, son of John, do you love Me?"

Peter, grieved, answered, "Lord, You know all things. You know that I love You."

Jesus nodded. "Feed My sheep."

Peter understood. His denial was forgiven. Jesus was restoring him, calling him once again—not to fishing, but to shepherding His people.

As the sun rose higher, Jesus reminded them, **"Do not worry about food or clothing. Seek first the kingdom of God, and all these things will be given to you."** He sent them out again—not as fishermen, but as preachers of the Good News.

The 153 fish remained in their memory—not just as a miracle, but as a sign of Jesus' provision and their calling to gather people from all nations into His kingdom.

From that day forward, Peter and his companions never turned back. They left their nets for good and became true fishers of men.

As Peter and the other disciples sat around the fire, their bellies full from the meal Jesus had prepared, their hearts still wrestled with doubt and fear. They had followed Jesus, witnessed His miracles, and heard His teachings. Yet, after everything—the betrayal, the crucifixion, and even His resurrection—they had returned to fishing.

Jesus looked at them with deep love and understanding. **"Peter, James, John, Thomas, Nathanael—you were not called to be fishermen anymore. I invited you to walk with Me, to learn, to witness, and to understand the kingdom of God."**

He gestured toward the net, still filled with **153 large fish.** **"Do you see this catch? When I first called you, I said I would make you fishers of men. This net filled with fish is not just about the sea—it is about the people of the world, of different nations and languages, waiting to hear the Good News. You are no longer to catch fish, but to gather souls into My kingdom."**

The disciples listened intently as Jesus continued.

"The world did not accept Me, and it will not accept you. Just as they hated Me, they will hate you. Just as they put Me to death, they will seek to do the same to you. But do not fear—just as the Father raised Me from the dead, so too will you have life everlasting."

He looked at Peter, His voice filled with both authority and compassion. **"Why have you returned to fishing? You are trained to be fishers of men. I have prepared you. Now it is time to go into the world and preach. Do not be afraid of dying—fear instead for those who do not yet know Me, so they do not face eternal separation from God."**

Then, Jesus reminded them of the number **153**, the miraculous catch they had just witnessed.

"This is My final instruction to you. Just as this net gathered many fish, you must now go and gather people for My kingdom. I will no longer be with you in the flesh, but My Spirit will guide you. Go, and do not look back."

The disciples knew then that their time of hesitation was over. The risen Lord had spoken. Their purpose was clear. From that moment, they left their nets behind—not for fish, but for souls.

And so, they went into the world, carrying the message of Jesus, never forgetting the lesson of the **153 fish**—a reminder that their calling was not of the sea, but of the kingdom of God.

ONE

A Conversation between the Father, the Son, and the Holy Spirit

> *Scene: The three persons of the Holy Trinity, Father, Son, and Holy Spirit, are gathered together in a moment of divine communion, reflecting on the profound significance of the number "one."*

The Father: [In a voice full of love and authority] "The number one has always been central to our plan for the salvation of mankind. It speaks to the oneness that we share—the unity of our will, our essence, and our purpose. As I declared in the beginning, 'Let there be light,' and so it was. We are one in the creation of all things, and even in the work of redemption, we remain united."

The Son: [With a gentle but firm tone, His voice full of grace] "Indeed, Father. I declared, 'I and My Father are one' (John 10:30). This oneness is not just in purpose, but in essence. I came to reveal that we are not separate—our power, our authority, our very being are intertwined. I did not come to act independently, but in perfect unity with You, to bring forth the Kingdom of Heaven."

The Holy Spirit: [Softly, but with a deep, resonant presence] "And when You, Son, ascended to the Father, You did not leave Your people without guidance. I was sent to dwell in them, to bring them into the fullness of our oneness. Those who trust in

You, who accept the call to follow, now experience our presence within them. Together, Father, Son, and Spirit, we unite with them to fulfill the divine mission."

The Father: [Nodding with affection] "Yes, my Spirit. You are the bond that unites us with the hearts of all who believe. The oneness we share becomes their oneness with us. It is through the Spirit that they are empowered to carry out the mission—one mission, one purpose, to bring the Good News to all the nations."

The Son: [His voice filled with conviction] "This mission is crucial. When I performed the miracle of the 153 fish (John 21:11), it wasn't just about a count. It was a message. That number reminds them that there is only one true God (Deuteronomy 6:4), only one path to salvation—through Me (John 14:6), and one calling to fulfill—to spread the Gospel. The number one echoes the singularity of purpose for those who follow."

The Holy Spirit: [With a deep sigh of understanding] "And through our unity, those who trust in You, Son, will find liberation. The number one, in its essence, signifies the trust they place in You. I, the Spirit, empower them to have faith that You have conquered all things—nature, sickness, life, and death. Those who trust in You will not be lost, but will receive eternal life in the Kingdom we have prepared."

The Father: [With a sense of finality and promise] "And at the end of time, Son, You will return, and all will be made new. A new heaven and a new earth will be established, perfectly united in our presence (Revelation 21:1). The separation caused by sin will be no more. All will be restored to perfect oneness with us, as it was meant to be from the beginning."

The Son: [With a loving, resolute tone] "Yes, Father. The fulfilment of our will, the unity of all things in heaven and on earth, will finally come to pass. Every person who trusts in the one true God will be part of this perfect restoration, where all is made new, and we dwell together, as we always have, in eternal unity."

The Holy Spirit: [With a quiet but certain assurance] "The number one, then, is not just a number—it is a call to all to see and embrace this unity. There is but one God, one path to salvation, and one mission for all who follow. It is a reminder to all believers: to trust in the oneness we share, to follow the one true way, and to fulfill the one great mission given to us."

The Father: [With a tender smile, His voice full of love] "Indeed, it is a call to the hearts of all who seek us, that in the oneness of our love, they find their purpose and their peace."

The Son: [Nodding with a deep sense of fulfillment] "May all who hear this call find their way in the oneness of the Father, the Son, and the Holy Spirit."

The Holy Spirit: [With a quiet, loving whisper] "For in that unity, they will find life, and life abundantly."

(The three of them are silent for a moment, fully at peace in their eternal unity, knowing the work they began is unfolding exactly as planned—one God, one path, one mission.)

FIVE

Scene: Adam, Solomon, and a modern-day scientist are sitting in a lush garden, surrounded by the beauty of creation. They are deep in conversation about the design and order of the universe.

Adam: [Looking around thoughtfully, his voice calm and filled with reverence] "When I first saw the world, it was a canvas of perfect harmony. The Creator spent five days bringing it all into being—each day shaping a part of this world, making it ready for life. The heavens, the earth, the seas, the stars... and the creatures that walked the earth. On the sixth day, He created me, in His own image. Everything was deliberate, each step leading to the creation of humanity. The number five—it seems to stand at the heart of it all."

Solomon: [With a wise gaze, nodding slowly] "Indeed, Adam. Five is more than just a number. It represents balance and divine perfection. The first five days of creation were a preparation for humanity, a foundation upon which the world was built. There is wisdom in the way the Creator designed everything, and the number five is woven into the very fabric of existence."

Scientist: [Adjusting his glasses, intrigued, leaning forward] "That's fascinating. From a scientific perspective, five seems to represent balance and stability, not just in creation, but in nature as well. The human hand, for example, has five fingers. It's not just for functionality, but for stability and efficiency. Each finger has a purpose—gripping, pointing, balancing. I'm starting to see how the number five plays a role in both the physical and spiritual realms."

Adam: [Looking at his hands, his voice filled with understanding] "Yes, I remember when I first saw my hands. The thumb represents strength, the foundation of life, like the parents who give us our beginnings. The index finger guides the way, like a sibling pointing the path. The middle finger is a reminder of oneself—standing firm in the center. The ring finger symbolizes the bond of love, the commitment of a spouse. And the little finger... so small, yet so precious, representing children—the future of our world. These five fingers remind me of the blessings of family, and how we are to love and care for one another."

Solomon: [With a deep and knowing smile] "The number five reflects the harmony of relationships—parental love, sibling bonds, self-awareness, marital unity, and the preciousness of children. Just as God taught, we are called to love one another with the same care and reverence as we cherish these relationships in our hands."

Scientist: [Nods thoughtfully, his curiosity piqued] "And it doesn't stop there. The number five shows up in nature and human innovation as well. A five-legged chair, for instance, is more stable than one with fewer legs. A ceiling fan with five blades circulates air more effectively than one with four or six.

It's as if the number five is a symbol of balance and strength, even in the design of everyday things."

Adam: [His face lighting up with recognition] "Yes! Even the physical world carries this balance. I've seen how the world is designed for stability—how each part of creation works together, complementing one another. The Creator made sure there was balance in everything. Even in the stars above, a five-pointed star has been used for centuries to symbolize guidance and divine protection."

Solomon: [With a solemn voice, gazing upwards] "In ancient times, we understood that numbers were not just tools for counting, but symbols of divine truth. The five-pointed star, the triangle over the square, represented the harmony between heaven and earth. The divine and the earthly were meant to work together, in balance, with one supporting the other. The number five, even in ancient symbolism, spoke of the perfection of creation."

Scientist: [Thoughtfully stroking his chin, a new perspective dawning on him] "I can see it now. The number five is more than just a mathematical concept. It's a part of the very design of creation—whether it's the stability of a five-legged chair or the balance of the human hand, the number five is a symbol of harmony. Even in our modern world, when we create, we are guided by principles of balance and symmetry, often unknowingly echoing the divine wisdom that shaped everything."

Adam: [Smiling warmly, his voice filled with conviction] "The Creator's wisdom is in every detail of His design. The world around us is filled with balance—physical, emotional, and spiritual. The number five teaches us that God has provided everything we need for life, and that balance is key to understanding the perfection of His creation."

Solomon: [With a deep, reflective tone] "Indeed. God's wisdom is perfect. His provision, His balance, and His order are reflected in the world we live in. The number five is a reminder of His divine plan—of how everything, from creation to relationships to the very structure of the universe, is woven together in perfect harmony. We are meant to live in balance, to care for one another, and to cherish the world He has entrusted to us."

Scientist: [Looking up at the sky, contemplative] "I never realized how much the number five ties into so much of what we see in nature and design. It's not just a number; it's a message—about balance, order, and the wisdom of creation. I see now how the Creator has imbued everything with His intelligence, His care, and His perfect plan."

Adam: [Looking back at the world around him, his voice soft but certain] "And as we reflect on the number five, let it remind us that in everything, there is balance. In the world, in our relationships, and in the way we live our lives. We are stewards of this creation, and it is our responsibility to nurture the balance He has established."

Solomon: [With a knowing look, his voice filled with ancient wisdom] "Indeed, the number five teaches us that perfection lies in balance. May we live with that understanding, in harmony with the Creator and with each other."

(The three of them sit in silence for a moment, reflecting on the divine wisdom woven into creation, the balance of the world, and the responsibility they carry in maintaining that harmony.)

THREE

A Conversation Between God, the Devil, and Man

Scene: A vast expanse beyond time—between heaven and earth. God stands in radiant light, the Devil lurks in the shadows, and Man stands between them, searching for truth.

1. The Holy Trinity – Three in One

God: [In a voice of authority, filled with love] "From the beginning, I have been three yet one—Father, Son, and Holy Spirit. I am not divided, but whole. My presence fills heaven and earth. The Son carries My love, and the Spirit moves among My people."

Man: [Curious, yet uncertain] "Three? But if You are one God, why three?"

God: [With patience] "The Father—Creator of all. The Son—Redeemer of all. The Holy Spirit—Guide and Comforter. Three, yet one. Like the past, present, and future—different, yet the same. Like water, which is ice, liquid, and vapor, yet remains water. This is My nature, a mystery beyond human wisdom."

Devil: [Scoffing, stepping forward] "Ah, but why should he believe? It's too complicated. Man seeks what he can see and touch. Why not let him rely on his own understanding?"

Man: [Looking between them, hesitant] "I want to believe, but it's hard to grasp."

God: [Gently] "Then walk with Me, and understanding will follow."

2. The Fall and the Need for Redemption

God: [Looking at Man, voice filled with sorrow] "I created you with free will, that you might choose love over rebellion. But in the garden, you turned away. And with that choice, sin entered the world."

Man: [Ashamed, looking down] "I know the story of Adam and Eve. They ate what You told them not to. But why did You let them?"

Devil: [Grinning] "Yes, tell him, God. Why give them a choice at all? If You loved them, why allow them to fail?"

God: [Firmly] "Because love is not love if it is forced. I gave them everything, yet they listened to the deceiver's lies."

Devil: [Laughing softly] "And they still do. Man loves his sin. He is weak, easily swayed. Just look at him! He falls, over and over again. Why bother trying to save him?"

Man: [With a troubled heart] "He's right... No matter how hard I try, I fail. Sin is everywhere. Even when I want to do good, I fall short."

God: [Looking at Man with love] "That is why I made a way. Sin brought death, but I brought life."

3. The Ultimate Sacrifice – Jesus Christ

God: [With deep compassion] "I did not leave you in darkness. No man could save himself, so I became flesh. My Son walked among you, bore your burdens, and took your punishment."

Man: [Whispering] "Jesus…"

Devil: [Scowling] "Ah yes, Jesus. The so-called Savior. But tell me, Man, did you see Him? Did you watch Him rise? How do you know it's true?"

Man: [Hesitant] "I… I don't know. It's been so long. How can I be sure?"

God: [Firmly] "Look at the cross. My Son suffered, was mocked, and crucified—not for His own sins, but for yours. He rose on the third day, conquering sin and death. It is written, and it is true."

Devil: [Sneering] "But does he really believe? Look at the world, God. Violence. Greed. Sin runs wild. Your 'sacrifice'—has it really changed anything?"

God: [With unwavering certainty] "Yes. Because for every soul that believes, the chains of sin are broken. My love does not force, it invites. And all who call on My name will be saved."

Man: [With newfound hope] "Then… I want to believe. I want to be free."

4. The Holy Spirit – Completing the Divine Plan

God: [With a voice full of promise] "You are not alone. I have sent My Spirit to dwell within those who believe—to guide, to strengthen, to remind you of My truth."

Man: [Eager, yet uncertain] "But what if I fall again?"

Devil: [Chuckling darkly] "Oh, you will fall. You always do. That's the beauty of it. You're too weak to follow God perfectly."

God: [Gently, yet firmly] "Yes, you may stumble. But My Spirit will lift you up. You will learn to walk in My strength, not your own."

Man: [With hope growing] "So I don't have to do this alone?"

God: [Smiling] "Never."

5. The Power of Three in God's Plan

God: [With wisdom beyond time] "Three is not just a number—it is a pattern of My design. It represents completion, redemption, and renewal."

Man: [Counting on his fingers] "Jesus rose on the third day… You revealed Yourself as Father, Son, and Holy Spirit… Peter denied You three times, and You restored him three times…"

God: [Nodding] "Yes. Three speaks of My work throughout time—past, present, and future. It speaks of My eternal nature and My plan to redeem and restore all things."

Devil: [Crossing his arms, irritated] "Hmph. But will Man remember? He is quick to forget. He runs to his doubts and fears the moment trials come."

Man: [Looking at God, determination in his eyes] "I don't want to forget. I want to live in the truth."

God: [With love and assurance] "Then hold fast to My Word. Walk in faith. And when doubts come, remember the power of three—My love, My sacrifice, and My Spirit within you."

Devil: [Scoffing, stepping back into the shadows] "Tch. We'll see how long that lasts."

Man: [Standing taller, hope shining in his eyes] "No… I know it will last. Because You are with me."

God: [With a radiant smile] "Always."

(The light grows brighter, and Man steps forward, leaving the shadows behind. The Devil watches from the distance, knowing he has lost yet another soul to the truth.)

The Divine Promise and the Sacred Journey of His People

Scene: A gathering under the shade of a great oak tree, in a peaceful valley near the ancient ruins of Babel. Noah, Moses, Abraham, and Jacob sit in contemplation, reflecting on the history of God's people and the divine plans that have unfolded through the ages. The sky is painted with the hues of twilight as they begin to speak.

Noah: [Looking towards the heavens, a solemn expression on his face] "In the days of old, when the earth was yet untainted, I heard the voice of the Lord. He spoke of cleansing the world, of washing away the wickedness that had soiled the beauty He had created. But I was chosen, called to build an ark—a vessel of salvation for my family, for those few who still knew His name. It is a heavy burden, to know that only those within the ark would survive. But, by His grace, I trusted. And the flood came. The earth was reborn, and in my heart, I knew that God's promise was true."

Moses: [Nods thoughtfully, his staff resting beside him] "Yes, Noah, you were faithful. But the journey of God's people did not end with the flood. Even after the waters receded, humanity still turned from the Lord. In the hardness of their hearts they built the Tower of Babel. They sought to climb to the heavens with their own hands, trying to make themselves equal to God. How prideful they were! But the Lord scattered them, giving them many languages, so they could no longer understand one another. It was His wisdom that saved them from their own arrogance."

Abraham: [A thoughtful smile crosses his face as he gazes into the distance] "I too was called by the Lord, Moses. I remember the day He spoke to me, calling me to leave my father's house and journey to a land He would show me. It was not easy, to leave behind all I knew, but I trusted His word. And in that trust, He promised me a legacy—'I will make thee a father of many nations,' He said. Through my descendants, all the families of the earth would be blessed. Little did I know then that His plan was much greater than I could fathom."

Jacob: [Leans forward, resting his hands on his knees, his voice filled with a quiet intensity] "Your journey, Abraham, was the beginning of something much grander. I remember when the Lord changed my name to Israel. I had wrestled with Him, uncertain, broken, but He gave me strength, and from me came the twelve tribes. I saw His faithfulness, even when we stumbled, even when we turned away. He called us His people, and He promised us a land flowing with milk and honey."

Moses: [With a deep sigh, recalling the wilderness] "Yet even with such promises, the people wandered. I led them through the desert, but their hearts remained distant. We were hungry, we were thirsty, and they grumbled, even though the Lord provided for us. He gave us manna from heaven and water from rocks. But it was never enough. Even then, He did not abandon us. He gave me the law, the Ten Commandments, to guide us—to teach us how to live in harmony with Him and with each other. 'Love the Lord your God with all your heart,' He said, 'and love your neighbor as yourself.' But how many times did we fail to do that?"

Noah: [With a gentle nod, his voice softening] "We failed many times, Moses. Even after the flood, the world has continued to turn its back on the Lord. But there has always been hope. The promise of redemption, the promise that God would send someone to save His people from themselves."

Abraham: [Looking up, a distant look in his eyes] "Yes, Noah. The promise of a Savior. I did not understand it fully, but I knew that it would come. And now, I see that God's plan has not only been for the Israelites but for all the nations of the earth. He would send His Son to redeem us all."

Moses: [His voice filled with reverence] "The Messiah. The One who would fulfill all the promises. He would lead us, not just out of Egypt, but out of sin and death itself. And the Lord would not just be our God, but the God of all people."

Jacob: [Sighs, a sense of peace settling over him] "It is strange, isn't it? The way the Lord works. He begins with one—Adam, then Noah, then Abraham—and through them, He forms a people. And now, through that people, He will bring salvation to the world. One man, one Savior, and all will be made right."

Noah: [Looking at the others with wisdom in his eyes] "Indeed, Jacob. But the journey has not been easy. It has been marked by struggle, by rebellion, and by grace. The world was cleansed through the flood, but even after that, mankind found a way to turn away. But the Lord's love is steadfast, His covenant unbroken. He has always provided a way for us to return to Him, even when we stray."

Abraham: [His face brightens with a sudden realization] "And now, through Jesus Christ, the Savior, all things will be restored. The promises that God gave to us, His people, will come to fruition. We were blessed to be a blessing, and through Jesus, the whole earth will be blessed."

Moses: [With a knowing look, his voice firm] "Yes. We have walked a long road, but it leads to Him. The Redeemer. And through Him, all will be made new."

Jacob: [With a gentle smile, a sense of hope filling his heart] "Indeed, Moses. And though our part in this story is now finished, the journey continues. For the Savior has come, and He will return. The covenant remains, and all who believe in Him will see the fulfilment of God's promises."

Noah: [With a deep breath, looking toward the stars] "And it is in Him, in that great promise of salvation, that we place our hope. For He will bring us home, to the land He has promised—a land where His love reigns forever."

Moses: [Nods in agreement] "Let us hold fast to that hope, and let the generations to come know that the God who called us, who redeemed us, is the same God who will bring all things to completion."

Abraham: [Looking at his descendants] "And His people shall be gathered from all the corners of the earth, from every nation and tribe. For His plan was always much greater than we could have imagined."

Jacob: [With a soft smile] "Yes, His plan is perfect, and in the end, His love will win."

(The four men sit together in the quiet evening, each reflecting on the journey that has brought them to this moment. The wind rustles through the trees, and the stars above shine brightly, a reminder of the promises of God that endure forever.)

A Conversation Between Isaiah, Jeremiah, and John the Baptist

Scene: A quiet wilderness, where the wind whispers through the trees. Three figures stand together—Isaiah, the visionary; Jeremiah, the weeping prophet; and John the Baptist, the voice crying in the wilderness. They have been given a moment beyond time to reflect on their shared mission: proclaiming the coming of the Messiah.

Isaiah: The Visionary of God's Glory

Isaiah: [Gazing into the distance, eyes filled with wonder] "I saw Him… high and exalted, seated on a throne, and the train of His robe filled the temple. The seraphim cried, 'Holy, holy, holy is the Lord Almighty!' And yet, this same glorious One was to be born as a child… a Son given to us, carrying the weight of our sins."

Jeremiah: [With sorrow in his voice] "And the people… did they believe your words?"

Isaiah: [Shaking his head] "Some listened, but many were blind, deaf to the truth. They expected a warrior king, yet I spoke of a suffering Servant—one who would be pierced for our transgressions, crushed for our iniquities. They did not understand that the way to victory was through sacrifice."

John: [Nodding in agreement] "They were not ready to hear it. Even in my day, they longed for a Messiah of power, not one of humility. But tell me, Isaiah, did you see the time when He would come?"

Isaiah: [With a knowing smile] "I saw glimpses—shadows of the future. A virgin would conceive and bear a Son, and His name would be called Immanuel… God with us."

Jeremiah: [Softly] "God… with us."

Jeremiah: The Weeping Prophet of Hope

Jeremiah: [Looking at Isaiah] "Your visions were grand, filled with majesty. But my days were filled with grief. The people turned from God, and my heart broke for them. I warned them of judgment, but they would not listen."

John: [With urgency] "Yet you also spoke of hope."

Jeremiah: [Nodding] "Yes… even in the darkness, there was hope. I saw the days when God would make a new covenant. No longer written on stone, but upon the hearts of His people. A covenant that would truly cleanse them from their sins."

Isaiah: [Reflecting] "And this covenant… it could only come through the sacrifice of the One I saw—the One who would be 'led like a lamb to the slaughter.'"

John: [Eyes lighting up] "The Lamb of God! That is what I called Him when I saw Him at the Jordan!"

Jeremiah: [Hope stirring in his heart] "Then... He has come?"

John: [Smiling, full of certainty] "Yes. And I had the privilege of preparing His way."

John the Baptist: The Voice Crying in the Wilderness

Isaiah: [Studying John] "Your voice... it was like a trumpet in the desert. You were the one crying out, 'Prepare the way of the Lord!'"

John: [Laughing slightly] "Yes, but they thought I was mad. A wild man in the wilderness, calling them to repentance. Yet, I knew my purpose—to go before Him, to make the path straight. When I saw Him, I knew. I told them, 'One is coming after me who is mightier than I, whose sandals I am not worthy to untie.'"

Jeremiah: [With awe] "And the people... did they believe?"

John: [Sighing] "Some. Many came to be baptized, confessing their sins. But others, the religious leaders... they hardened their hearts. They feared losing their power."

Isaiah: [Grimly] "They did not understand that the Messiah's kingdom was not of this world."

John: [With fire in his voice] "But I knew. I told them—'Behold, the Lamb of God, who takes away the sin of the world!' And yet..." [His voice grows quiet] "...they did not all receive Him."

The Prophetic Tapestry

Jeremiah: [Looking between Isaiah and John] "Our messages were different, yet they all pointed to the same truth. A King would come, a Shepherd for His people, a Lamb for their sacrifice."

Isaiah: [Softly] "A Servant who would suffer... yet reign forever."

John: [Firmly] "And I saw Him with my own eyes."

Isaiah: [With awe] "Then the words God gave us were fulfilled."

Jeremiah: [Hopeful, despite his past sorrows] "And the covenant I spoke of... it has begun?"

John: [Nodding] "Yes. Through His blood, He has made a way. No longer will the law be written on stone, but on the hearts of those who believe."

Isaiah: [Smiling] "Then truly, He is Immanuel—God with us."

Jeremiah: [Hope shining in his eyes] "And He will gather His people... not just Israel, but all who believe in His name."

John: [With conviction] "The Kingdom of God has come. And though they took my life, I know—He will reign forever."

(The three prophets stand in silent reflection, their voices now woven into the great tapestry of redemption. They had spoken the words given to them, and now, in the fullness of time, the Messiah had fulfilled them. Their hearts are at peace, knowing that their mission was not in vain, for the Light of the World had come.)

The Gathering of Five: A Conversation Across Time

Scene: The moon, like a silver sentinel, casts its gentle glow upon five women seated beneath an ancient olive tree. Their faces, radiant with wisdom and grace, bear the marks of journeys woven into the sacred fabric of history. They have been summoned beyond the veil of time to speak of the wondrous tapestry of divine providence—a lineage that led to the birth of the Savior.

Tamar: The Flame of Justice
With eyes deep as twilight and a voice steady as the rivers of old, Tamar speaks first.

"Mine is a tale of patience and divine reckoning. Betrayed and discarded, I wore the veil of deception not in malice, but in faith, that the name of Judah would not be extinguished. I endured disgrace so that a promise might live. And when the time of unveiling came, I was declared righteous. Through my womb, Perez and Zerah took their first breath, and thus the line of kings continued."

Rahab: The Scarlet Thread of Redemption
A woman of striking presence, Rahab folds her hands upon her lap, her voice imbued with both humility and strength.

"I was once called unclean, a woman of the night. But my ears had heard of the wonders of the Almighty, and my heart trembled before His power. When the men of Israel sought refuge, I chose to shelter them, and in return, I was given a new name among the people of God. A scarlet cord, a symbol of salvation, hung from my window, and in that thread, I found redemption. From me came Boaz, a man of kindness, whose own love would weave into the grand design of eternity."

Ruth: The Harvest of Love
Ruth, her countenance gentle as morning dew, bows her head in reverence before she speaks.

"I was a stranger, a daughter of Moab, yet love bound me to the people of Israel. 'Where you go, I will go; where you stay, I will stay. Your people shall be my people, and your God, my God.' These words became my covenant, and through them, I walked the fields of Bethlehem, gleaning not just grain, but a destiny far greater than my own. I was but a lowly widow, yet the Lord clothed me in honor, placing me in the lineage of David, the shepherd-king."

Bathsheba: The Queen of Sorrow and Strength
Her eyes, like pools reflecting both sorrow and splendor, Bathsheba lifts her face to the stars.

"My tale is whispered in hushed tones, marked by shadows and sorrow. I was taken, my life entangled with a king's folly, and the weight of it nearly crushed me. But the Lord, in His mercy, turned mourning into purpose. From my womb came Solomon, a king clothed in wisdom. And from his line, another King would rise, One who would reign not with chariots and swords, but with love everlasting."

Mary: The Vessel of Grace
The youngest among them, yet adorned with a serenity beyond years, Mary places her hands upon her heart as she speaks.

"The angel came to me, and his words were as a river of light—'Rejoice, highly favored one, the Lord is with you!' How could I, a simple maiden of Nazareth, be chosen for such a wonder? Yet, I bowed to His will, and in my womb, the Word became flesh. The One whom you all have longed for, the One whispered of in prophecy—He came, not in robes of majesty, but in swaddling cloths, resting in a manger. Through Him, the broken are made whole, the lost are found, and the promise is fulfilled."

A Tapestry Woven in Grace

A hush falls upon them, each woman gazing at the other with understanding that transcends time. Their stories, once scattered like seeds upon the wind, have taken root in the grand design of the Almighty. They are bound together—not by birth, not by nation, but by the divine hand that guided them each to their purpose.

Tamar, the flame of justice. Rahab, the scarlet thread of redemption. Ruth, the harvest of love. Bathsheba, the queen of sorrow and strength. And Mary, the vessel of grace. Through them, the Savior came, and through Him, all are made new.

The wind stirs the olive branches above them, as if heaven itself whispers its approval. They smile, knowing their journeys were never in vain. For in the heart of eternity, their names are written—not as mere footnotes of history, but as heralds of salvation.

The Profound Significance of the Number Five in Jesus' Ministry

The disciples are gathered around Jesus as they rest after ministering to the crowds. The sun begins to set, casting golden hues over the hills of Galilee. They have just witnessed the miraculous feeding of the five thousand, and their hearts are full of wonder.

Peter: Master, today we saw a miracle beyond our understanding. With only five loaves and two fish, You fed thousands! How can this be?

Jesus: (smiling) My dear Peter, do you not see? The bread and fish were but a sign of the greater provision that comes from the Father. Man does not live by bread alone but by every word that proceeds from the mouth of God. The number five, woven into this miracle, is a symbol of My provision and power.

John: Rabbi, I have heard the number five carries deep meaning in the Scriptures. Could You tell us more?

Jesus: Indeed, John. Consider the five fears that often grip the hearts of men: the fear of hunger, the fear of disease, the fear of evil, the fear of nature's fury, and the fear of death. Yet, have I not shown you that none of these can stand before the authority given to Me by the Father?

Andrew: (thoughtfully) Yes, Lord. Today, You met the hunger of the people. You have also healed the sick and cast out demons. I remember when You calmed the storm that frightened us. And Lazarus… You called him forth from the grave. Truly, nothing is beyond Your power!

Jesus: You have spoken rightly, Andrew. The Father sent Me not only to perform miracles but to reveal that in Me, there is no lack. The bread multiplied today is but a shadow of the true Bread that I offer—the Bread of Life. Whoever comes to Me shall never hunger, and whoever believes in Me shall never thirst.

Philip: Master, even the twelve baskets left over—what do they mean?

Jesus: (gently) They signify the abundance of God's kingdom, Philip. The twelve tribes of Israel, the twelve who walk with Me—you will carry My message, and there will always be more than enough for all who seek Me. My grace is boundless.

Matthew: (pausing) Rabbi, the number five also reminds me of the five wise virgins in Your parable. They were prepared with oil for their lamps, while the other five were not. Is there a connection?

Jesus: (nodding) Yes, Matthew. Just as the five loaves sustained the multitude, so too must your faith be sustained. The wise virgins kept their lamps burning, ready for the Bridegroom's arrival. Be vigilant, for the Son of Man will come at an hour you do not expect. Keep the oil of faith burning in your hearts.

Thomas: Lord, You have spoken of five fears, but what of our hands? Each of us has five fingers on each hand. Is there meaning in this?

Jesus: (smiling warmly) Indeed, Thomas. The hands of man were made to labor, to give, and to receive. With these hands, the sick are healed, the hungry are fed, and burdens are lifted. But soon, My hands will bear the wounds of the cross—five wounds, given for the salvation of many. These hands, pierced for you, will forever be a sign of My love.

(The disciples fall silent, pondering the depth of His words. The fire crackles softly as the night descends.)

Jesus: (looking at them with deep love) My friends, do not fear, for I am with you. I have come to fulfill the will of My Father. Trust in Me, and in time, you will understand all things. For now, rest in My peace, and know that the provision of today is but a glimpse of the eternal feast that awaits those who believe.

(The disciples bow their heads, filled with reverence. Though they do not fully grasp His words, they feel the weight of their truth. The night deepens, but in their hearts, the light of Christ burns ever brighter.)

The Significance of the Number Three in the Ministry of Jesus

The scene is set on a quiet evening as Peter, James, and John sit together, reflecting on all they have witnessed. The warmth of a small fire flickers between them as they speak.

Peter: Brethren, I cannot stop thinking about the significance of the number three in our Lord's ministry. The way He chose to reveal Himself in divine moments—again and again, threefold. It was not by accident; it was always part of His perfect plan.

James: Aye, Peter. From the very beginning, He chose the three of us to witness the most sacred moments of His life. The mountaintop—when we saw Him transfigured before our eyes—still fills me with awe.

John: I remember it well. His face shone like the sun, His robes whiter than anything of this earth. And then Moses and Elijah stood with Him! It was as if the fullness of the Law and the Prophets pointed directly to Him as the fulfillment of all things.

Peter: And yet, we could hardly grasp it at that moment. I foolishly spoke of building shelters for them, as if that fleeting moment could be contained! But then, the voice of the Father thundered from the heavens, saying, This is my beloved Son; listen to Him!

James: That moment was meant to prepare us, though we did not fully understand at the time. And how often He performed His greatest miracles in patterns of three! Three times, He raised the dead to life: the widow's son in Nain, Jairus' daughter, and Lazarus. Each time, death obeyed His voice.

John: I remember the weeping of Jairus when he feared all was lost. But Jesus told him to believe. And when He took her by the hand and said, Little girl, arise, life returned to her in an instant. It was a glimpse of what was to come.

Peter: And Lazarus… his resurrection foreshadowed the greatest miracle of all. Our Lord waited until the third day, and when He called Lazarus forth, death had no hold on him. It was as if Jesus was preparing us for His own victory over the grave.

James: We should have seen it, Peter. He told us so many times that He would be handed over, crucified, and rise again on the third day. But our hearts were slow to understand.

John: And yet, He fulfilled it just as He said. Three days in the tomb—and then the stone was rolled away! Oh, what joy filled my heart when I ran to the empty tomb! The grave could not hold Him!

Peter: And do you remember how He restored me after I denied Him? Three times, He asked me, Do you love Me? Three times, I answered, and three times, He commanded me to tend His sheep. I had failed Him, but in His mercy, He restored me completely.

James: It seems the number three was woven into everything. Even as He hung upon the cross, three hours of darkness covered the land. And at the third hour, He breathed His last, completing His sacrifice for us all.

John: The fullness of God's plan was revealed through Him. Three persons in one God—Father, Son, and Holy Spirit. Three days in the grave before His resurrection. Three of us at His transfiguration. And now, we go forth, carrying the message of His salvation to the ends of the earth.

Peter: Indeed, brethren. We were privileged to witness His glory, to see His power over life and death, and to receive His commission. The number three was not just a pattern; it was a sign of the completeness of His work.

James: And soon, we shall see Him again. He ascended before our eyes, but He promised to return. Just as He rose on the third day, so shall He come again in glory.

John: Until then, we must be faithful. The number three is a reminder to us—of His power, His promise, and our mission. Let us proclaim His name with boldness, for He is the Way, the Truth, and the Life.

(The three disciples sit in reverent silence, their hearts full of faith, as the fire crackles softly. The weight of their mission is clear, but so is their hope. The story of Jesus is far from over—it is only beginning.)

The Divine Significance of Numbers 1, 3, and 5 in the Ministry of Jesus' Disciples

In the grand unfolding of God's divine plan, the numbers one, three, and five shine like guiding stars in the ministry of Jesus and His disciples, each carrying a sacred message that echoes the power, grace, and completeness of God's work on earth. These numbers, woven into the very fabric of the disciples' journey, reveal profound truths that transcend time, calling believers to a deeper understanding of God's purpose and the spiritual truths they embody.

The Power of One: The Unity and Authority of God's Kingdom

The number one stands as a beacon of unity and singular purpose in the ministry of Jesus and His disciples. God is one, and so too is His mission through Christ—a mission of redemption for all mankind. When Jesus imparted His healing power to His disciples, He bestowed upon them the divine authority to heal the sick, raise the dead, and proclaim the message of eternal life. This power, though channeled through His disciples, was never divided, for it flowed from the singular source of Jesus Himself—the one true God, who sent His Son to bring salvation to the world.

In the healing and miracles performed by His disciples, Jesus' divine power was unmistakably present. It was through one name—the name of Jesus—that they could accomplish these mighty works. Peter, ever faithful to his Lord, demonstrated this authority in Acts 9:30-43 when he raised Tabitha from the dead in the name of Jesus. The one name of Jesus was enough to conquer death and restore life. In this, we see the oneness of Jesus' divine mission—He came to bring life, to unite all things, and to restore what was lost.

The Power of Three: The Fullness of God's Revelation

The number three carries the weight of divine completeness, a symbol of God's perfect will and His revelation to the world. It is no coincidence that many significant moments in the ministry of Jesus and His disciples occurred in threes, echoing the triune nature of God—the Father, the Son, and the Holy Spirit. In this sacred number, we see the fullness of God's work, a work that is completed in Christ and manifested through His disciples.

One of the most poignant demonstrations of the threefold significance in the ministry of Jesus' disciples can be found in Peter's vision in Acts 10. When Peter was called to preach the gospel to the Gentiles, a divine vision was given to him in which a sheet filled with unclean animals descended from heaven. Three times this vision occurred, each time calling Peter to rise, kill, and eat. In each instance, Peter denied the command, but Jesus responded, "Do not call anything impure that God has made clean." This threefold repetition was not just a test of Peter's obedience but also a profound lesson in the universality of the gospel message. The number three here reflects the completeness of God's grace, which was now available not only to the Jews but to all people, transcending all boundaries. Moreover, the number three was intimately connected to the restoration of Peter's own soul. After his denial of Christ, Jesus appeared to him on the shore of the Sea of Galilee. In this intimate moment of healing and reconciliation, Jesus asked Peter three times, "Do you love Me?" Each affirmation of love was met with a commission to "feed My sheep," symbolizing the restoration of Peter's ministry and his place as a leader among the disciples. This threefold affirmation was not just for Peter's sake but for all believers, showing that no matter how many times we falter, God's grace is abundant and sufficient for us to rise again.

The Power of Five: The Extending Grace of the Gospel

The number five holds a special place in the ministry of Jesus, symbolizing grace, abundance, and the extension of God's mercy to all corners of the earth. It was through the disciples that Jesus' message would be spread far and wide, from Jerusalem to the ends of the earth. The number five is a reminder of the abundant grace and gifts that God has given to His followers to carry out His work in the world.

This is evident in the miraculous event where Jesus fed five thousand men with five loaves of bread and two fish, a beautiful symbol of God's provision and His desire to meet the needs of His people. But this act of multiplication also speaks to the grace that Jesus bestowed upon His disciples, empowering them to continue His mission of mercy and healing. It is through the grace of God that His disciples could heal the sick, raise the dead, and proclaim the gospel to all who would listen. In Acts 20:9-12, we see Peter continuing this legacy of grace. When a young boy named Eutychus fell from a window and was found dead, Peter, empowered by the Holy Spirit, raised him back to life. This miraculous act of grace extended the very gift of life itself to the boy and was a sign that the ministry of Jesus, through His disciples, would continue to bring restoration and healing to the world.

The Divine Harmony of One, Three, and Five

In the ministry of Jesus and His disciples, the numbers one, three, and five converge in a divine harmony that reveals the perfection of God's redemptive plan. The one name of Jesus, the singular source of all power and authority, brings healing, restoration, and salvation to the world. The threefold revelation of God's grace, as demonstrated in the repeated visions, the restoration of Peter, and the triune nature of God, speaks to the completeness and universality of God's message. And the number five, the number of grace, extends God's mercy and provision to all people, ensuring that His gospel reaches every corner of the earth.

These numbers are not merely mathematical; they are spiritual signposts that point to the nature of God's kingdom and the work of His disciples. Through these numbers, we see the abundance of God's grace, the fullness of His revelation, and the unity of His divine purpose. Just as Jesus sent His disciples to preach the message of everlasting life,

He also empowered them with the divine authority to heal, to raise the dead, and to proclaim the good news of salvation to all. And through the power of one, three, and five, the legacy of Jesus' ministry continues to echo throughout the ages, calling all believers to partake in the divine mission of grace, healing, and redemption.

Symbolism of 153

The meaning behind the 153 fish in John 21:11 has been widely discussed, with different interpretations from biblical scholars, historians, and theologians. Here are a few possible explanations:

1. A Symbol of All Nations and Languages

One interpretation suggests that the number 153 represents the nations and languages into which the Gospel must be preached. Some early scholars believed that at the time of Jesus, there were 153 known nations or ethnic groups in the world. This could symbolize the universality of Jesus' command to "go and make disciples of all nations" (Matthew 28:19).

- The five disciples fishing (Peter, Thomas, Nathanael, James, and John) could symbolize the mission of preaching to the five major regions or continents (Asia, Africa, Europe, America, and Australia).
- The five major languages (Egyptian, Greek, Hebrew, Aramaic, and Chinese) could represent the linguistic diversity in spreading the Gospel.
- Since Moses wrote the first books of the Bible in Hebrew and Egyptian, it shows that God's Word has always been meant to be shared across different cultures and languages.

2. Theological Symbolism of 153

Some believe that 153 is a symbolic number with mathematical and spiritual significance:

- 1 + 5 + 3 = 9, which is associated with divine completeness (as in the fruits of the Spirit in Galatians 5:22-23).
- 153 is the sum of the first 17 numbers (1+2+3...+17), and 17 is seen as a combination of 10 (God's law) and 7 (spiritual perfection).

3. Jesus' Call to Be Fishers of Men

Jesus had already told Peter and the others that they would become fishers of men (Matthew 4:19). The miraculous catch of 153 fish could be a direct confirmation that they were to bring people from all nations into God's kingdom, just as they had gathered the fish into their net.

Conclusion: The Most Likely Meaning

While the exact meaning of 153 is uncertain, the most commonly accepted explanation is that it represents the universal call to preach the Gospel to all people, nations, and languages. Jesus' final instruction to His disciples was to spread His message worldwide—which they did, and today, the Gospel continues to reach people across all continents and languages.

The 153 great fish, drawn from the depths of the sea, were not merely a bounty for hungry fishermen—they were a divine sign, a sacred commission entrusted to five chosen men. These were not just fishers of the sea but soon to be fishers of souls, sent forth to cast the net of salvation upon the vast waters of the world.

With divine intention, Jesus appeared before these five disciples, His presence radiant with purpose. He turned to Peter, His voice carrying the weight of eternity, and asked, "Will you carry My message? Will you take the Good News into the world?"

For even in numbers, there was meaning. The 153 was no accident, for Jesus, in His infinite wisdom, had woven its significance into His teaching. "I and My Father are one," He had declared, revealing the divine unity that bore the power of eternal life. The call to proclaim salvation was not meant for one people, nor one nation, but for every soul upon the five great continents of the earth.

No tongue would stand as a barrier, for just as the wind carries the fragrance of blooming flowers across distant lands, so too would the Spirit of God carry His Word into every language. And so it was on the day of Pentecost, when flames of fire danced upon the heads of His disciples, and the multitudes heard the Gospel in their own tongues (Acts 2:6-11).

Yet Jesus, knowing their hearts, reassured them. "Do not fear," He said, "for I am going to My Father. In His house are many mansions, and I go to prepare a place for you. But I shall return, and when I do, I will gather you to Myself, so that where I am, there you may be also" (John 14:2-3).

And so, the charge was given. The net was cast—not for fish, but for the hearts of men. And those who would lay down their lives for Him would find not death, but eternal life, dwelling forever in the presence of the Father.

About the Author

Dr. Sushil Dwyer is an accomplished Engineer from Kansas State University with several patents to his name in the field of Agricultural Engineering, notably the 'Threshing Assembly for a Combine'.

Born in Patna, a small town in India, Sushil grew to high positions in a Christian Engineering University in India before moving to the United States and worked at Deere & Company amongst others. Sushil is blessed with four sons and six grandchildren, loves writing for the glory of Jesus Christ and is settled in Greer, South Carolina with his loving wife, Avis.

Sushil is grateful to God for all His blessings throughout his life and now dedicates all his time speaking and writing about the goodness of God.

Made in the USA
Columbia, SC
30 March 2025